The Five Senses

Hearing

Rebecca Rissman

Heinemann Library
Chicago, Illinois

www.heinemannraintree.com
Visit our website to find out
more information about
Heinemann-Raintree books.

To order:
☎ Phone 888-454-2279
🖳 Visit www.heinemannraintree.com
to browse our catalog and order online.

© 2010 Heinemann Library
an imprint of Capstone Global Library, LLC
Chicago, Illinois

Edited by Rebecca Rissman and Catherine Veitch
Designed by Ryan Frieson and Kimberly R. Miracle
Original illustrations © Capstone Global Library
Illustrated by Tony Wilson (pp. 10, 22, 23)
Picture research by Tracy Cummins
Originated by Heinemann Library
Printed in China by South China Printing Company Ltd

14 13 12 11 10
10 9 8 7 6 5 4 3 2 1

Library of Congress Cataloging-in-Publication Data
Hearing / Rebecca Rissman.
p. cm. -- (The five senses)
ISBN 978-1-4329-3680-8 (hc) -- ISBN 978-1-4329-3686-0 (pb)
QP462.2.R57 2010
612.8'5--dc22
                          2009022287

Acknowledgments
The author and publishers are grateful to the following for permission
to reproduce copyright material: Age Fotostock pp. **9** (© Raymond
Forbes), **18** (© George Doyle), **23 C** (© George Doyle); Alamy p. **5**
(© Deco Images); AP Photo p. **20** (Al Behrman); Getty Images
pp. **7** (Xavier Bonghi), **11** (Jupiter Images), **12** (Regine Mahaux), **16**
(DreamPictures), **19** (Lise Metzger); istockphoto p. **13** (Plougmann);
Photolibrary pp. **6** (Frederic Cirou), **21** (Pawel Libera), **23 B** (Pawel
Libera); Shutterstock pp. **4** (© Maxim Slugin), **8** (© Ervin Monn), **14**
(© Sonya Etchison), **15** (© Steve Mann), **17** (© Muellek), **19 inset**
(© Jim Barber), **23 D** (© Maxim Slugin).

Cover photograph of a man whispering in a woman's ear reproduced
with permission of Getty Images (David Malan). Back cover photograph
of boys whispering reproduced with permission of Shutterstock (©
Sonya Etchison).

The publishers would like to thank Nancy Harris, Yael Biederman, and
Matt Siegel for their assistance in the preparation of this book.

Every effort has been made to contact copyright holders of any material
reproduced in this book. Any omissions will be rectified in subsequent
printings if notice is given to the publisher.

Contents

Senses

We all have five senses.

We use our senses every day.

Hearing and seeing are senses.

Tasting, smelling, and touching
are senses.

How Do You Hear?

ear

You use your ears to hear sound.

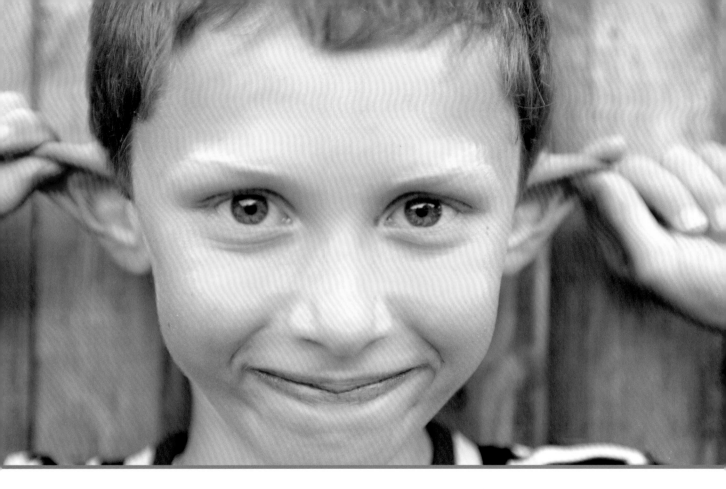

Your ears are on your head.

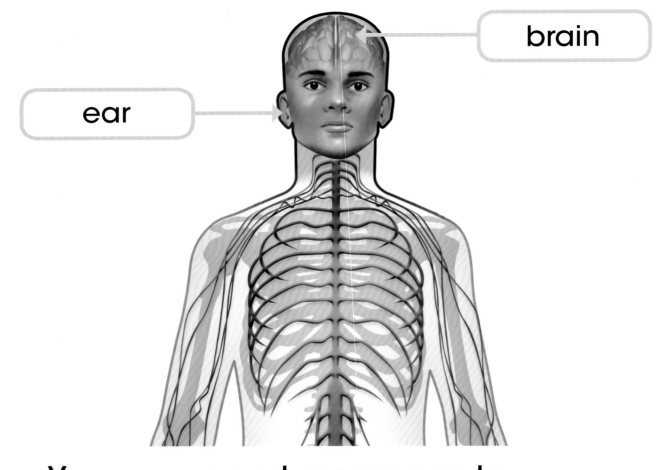

brain

ear

Your ears send messages to your brain.

Your brain tells you what you
are hearing.

What Can You Hear?

Your ears can hear loud sounds.

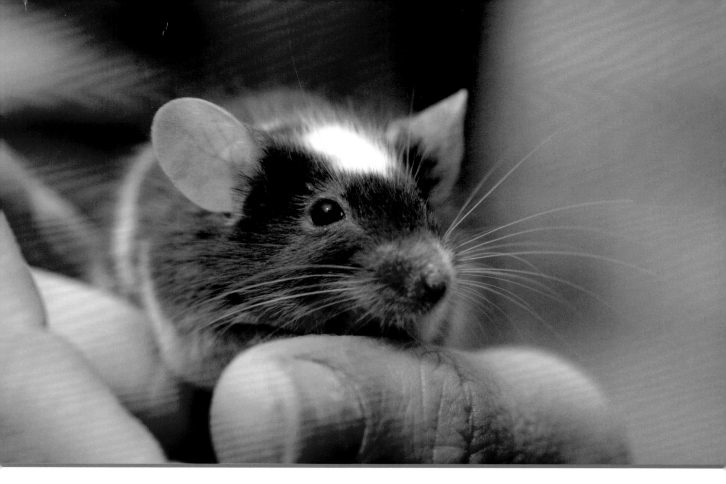

Your ears can hear quiet sounds.

Your ears can hear sounds that are close.

Your ears can hear sounds that are far away.

Your ears can hear high sounds.

Your ears can hear low sounds.

Protecting Your Ears

Do not stand close to very
loud sounds.

Do not put things into your ears.

Helping People Hear

Some people do not hear well.
They read hand signs.

hearing aid

Some people need hearing aids
to hear.

Naming the Parts You Use to Hear

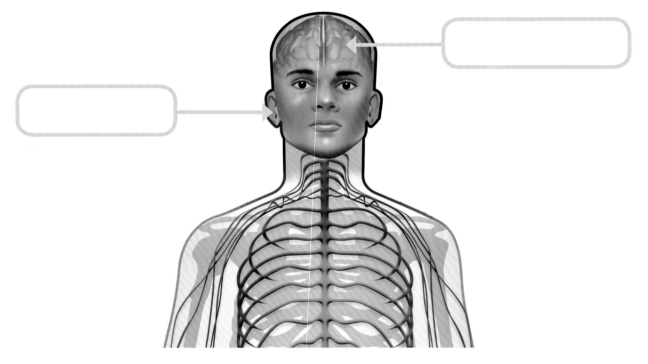

Point to where these labels should go.

brain   ear

Answer on page 10.

Picture Glossary

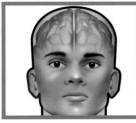

brain part of your body that helps you think, remember, feel, and move

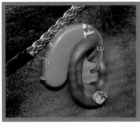

hearing aid small machine that helps people hear. Hearing aids fit inside and behind the ear.

protect keep something or someone safe

sense something that helps you smell, see, touch, taste, and hear things around you

Index

Note to Parents and Teachers

Before reading
Explain to children that people use five senses to understand the world: seeing, hearing, tasting, touching, and smelling. Tell children that there are different body parts associated with each sense. Then ask children which body part they think they use to hear. Tell children that they use their ears to hear.

After reading
• Ask children why they think people have two ears. Have children form pairs, and have one child close her eyes. Then ask the partner to make quiet sounds outside one of the child's ears. Ask the children if they think that having two ears helps them to detect where sound comes from.

• Show children the diagram of the ear on page 22. Ask them to point to where the labels "ear" and "brain" should go.

• Ask the children to sit in a circle and place a selection of objects that make different sounds in the centre of the circle. Tell all the children except one to shut their eyes and cover their eyes with their hands. Ask the child who can see to select one of the objects and make a sound with it. Can the other children guess the object?